D0574429

CRABTREE CONTACT

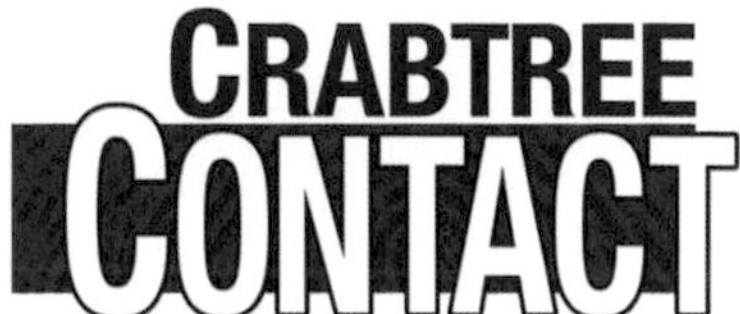

CRIME LAB TECHNICIAN

JOHN TOWNSEND

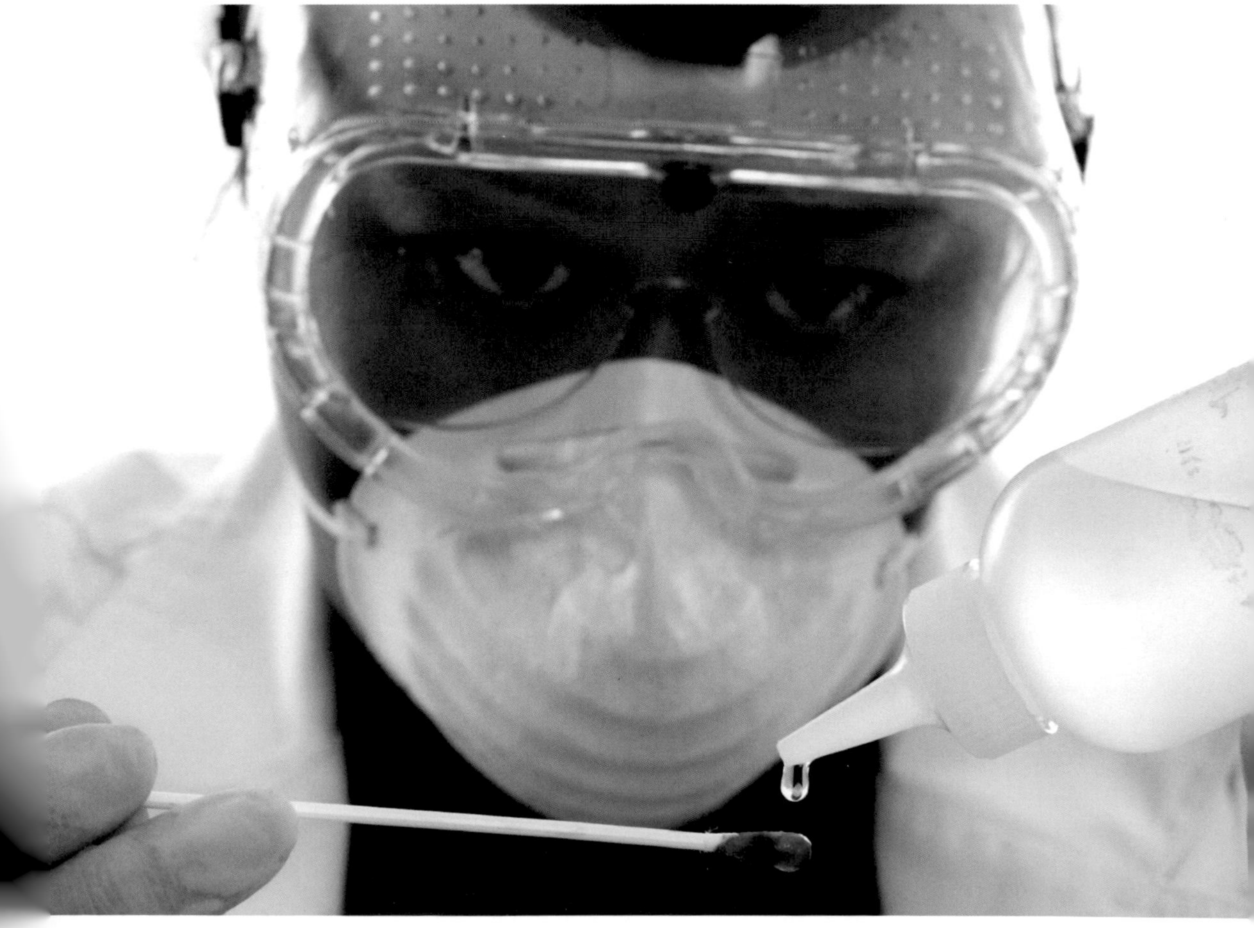

Crabtree Publishing Company

www.crabtreebooks.com

Crabtree Publishing Company
PMB 16A,
350 Fifth Avenue,
Suite 3308
New York, NY 10118

616 Welland Avenue,
St. Catharines, Ontario
L2M 5V6

Content development by
Shakespeare Squared

www.ShakespeareSquared.com

Published by Crabtree Publishing Company © 2008

First published in Great Britain in 2008 by ticktock Media Ltd,
2 Orchard Business Centre,
North Farm Road,
Tunbridge Wells, Kent, TN2 3XF

ticktock project editor:
Ruth Owen
ticktock project designer:
Sara Greasley
ticktock picture researcher:
Lizzie Knowles

Library and Archives Canada Cataloguing in Publication

Townsend, John, 1955-
Crime lab technician / John Townsend.

(Crabtree contact)
Includes index.

ISBN 978-0-7787-3807-7 (bound).--
ISBN 978-0-7787-3829-9 (pbk.)

1. Crime laboratories--Juvenile literature. 2. Criminal investigation--Vocational guidance--Juvenile literature. 3. Forensic sciences--Vocational guidance--Juvenile literature. 4. Crime scene searches--Juvenile literature. 5. Evidence, Criminal--Juvenile literature. I. Title. II. Series.

HV8073.8.T69 2008 j363.25'6 C2008-901213-5

With thanks to: Series Editors Honor Head and Jean Coppendale and Consultant John Cassella, Principal Lecturer in Forensic Science, Department of Forensic Science, Staffordshire University, UK

Picture credits (t=top; b=bottom; c=centre; l=left; r=right):
Peter Arnold, Inc./ Alamy: 21. Denis Closon/ Rex Features: 9, 16. Eye of Science/ Science Photo Library: 22, 25t, 25bl. Mauro Fermariello/ Science Photo Library: 5, 8, 14b. Steve Gschmeissner/ Science Photo Library: 18, 19. istock: 4tr, 20l, 23b, 24 inset, 28r, 24br. Jupiter Images/ Goodshoot: 27t. Mikael Karlsson/ Alamy: 14t. Richard Levine/ Alamy: 6b. David Parker/ Science Photo Library: 11. Photolibrary/ fstop: 26/27. Philippe Psaila/ Science Photo Library: 24. David Scharf/ Science Photo Library: 7 all. Shutterstock: OFC, 1, 2, 4tl, 6t, 10, 12/13, 16 inset, 17 all, 28l, 29, 31c. Superstock: 15, 23t. Andrew Syred/ Science Photo Library: 25br.

Every effort has been made to trace copyright holders, and we apologize in advance for any omissions. We would be pleased to insert the appropriate acknowledgments in any subsequent edition of this publication.

Library of Congress Cataloging-in-Publication Data

Townsend, John, 1955-
Crime lab technician / John Townsend.
p. cm. -- (Crabtree contact)
Includes index.
ISBN-13: 978-0-7787-3829-9 (pbk. : alk. paper)
ISBN-10: 0-7787-3829-9 (pbk. : alk. paper)
ISBN-13: 978-0-7787-3807-7 (reinforced library binding : alk. paper)
ISBN-10: 0-7787-3807-8 (reinforced library binding : alk. paper)
1. Criminal investigation--Vocational guidance--Juvenile literature. 2. Forensic sciences--Vocational guidance--Juvenile literature. 3. Crime laboratories--United States--Vocational guidance--Juvenile literature. 4. Crime scene searches--Juvenile literature. 5. Evidence, Criminal--Juvenile literature. I. Title. II. Series.
HV8073.8.T678 2008
363.25'6--dc22

2008006293

Content

CHAPTER 1

IT'S MURDER!

The police find a dead body in a room. The **victim** was shot!

The police talk to the victim's family, friends, and neighbors, and also to any **witnesses**.

Suspect A

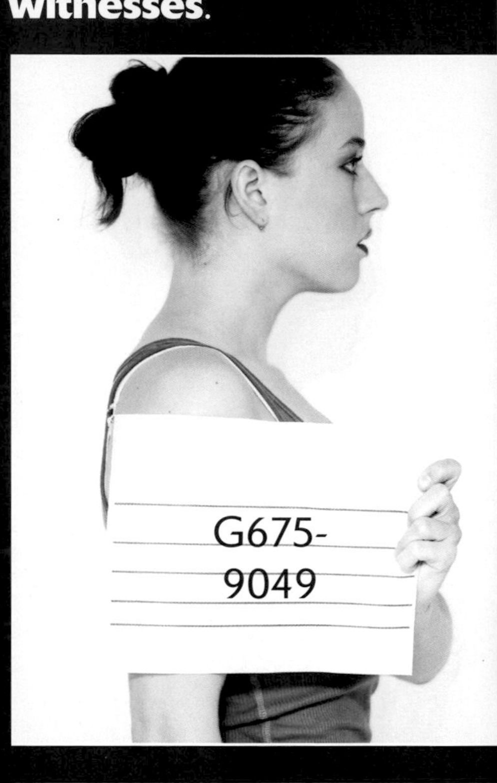

Suspect B

The police arrest two people. Both **suspects** say they know each other but they don't know the victim.

The police must find **evidence** to prove if the suspects are telling the truth or not.

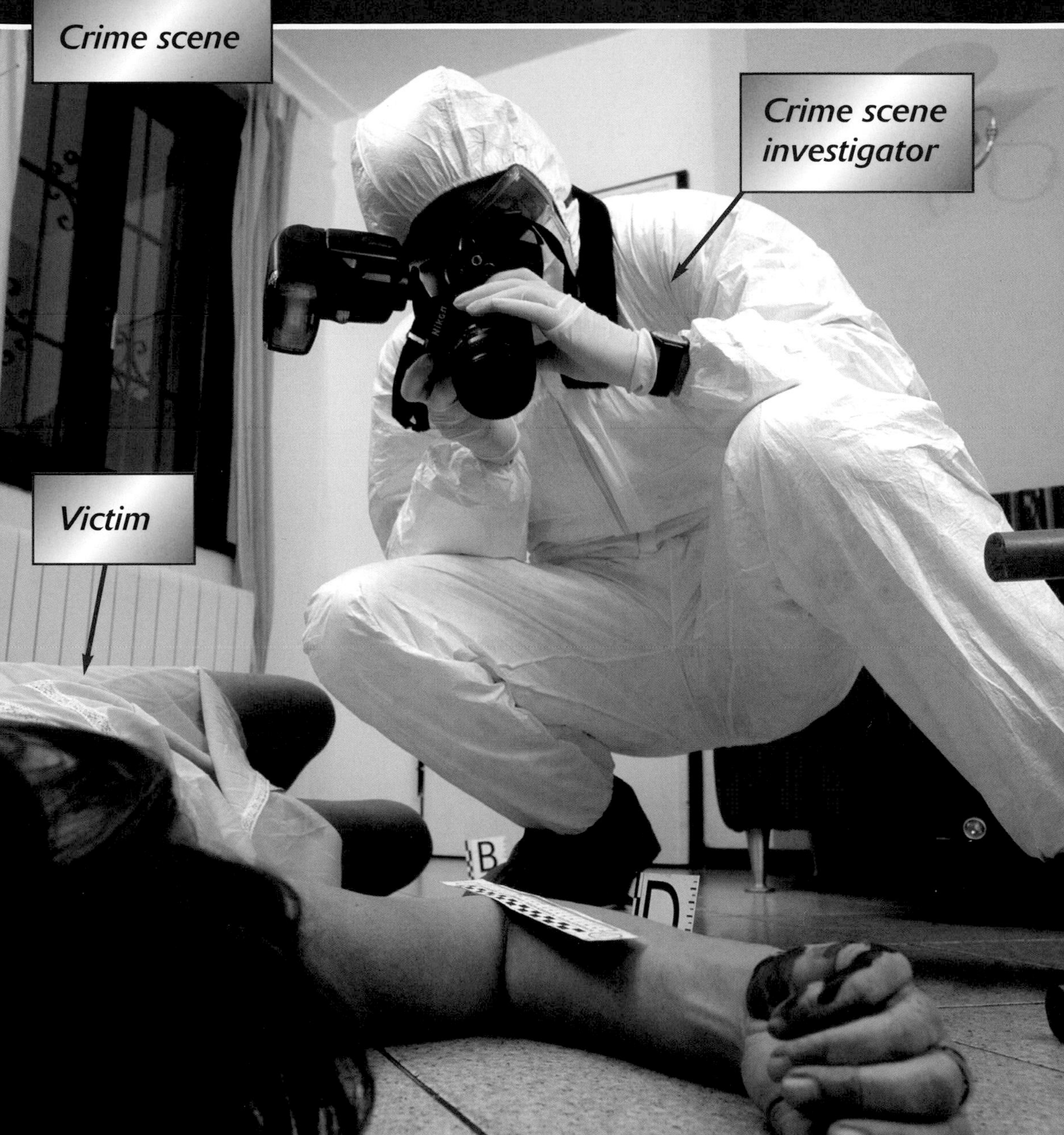

Crime Scene Investigators (CSIs) look for evidence at **crime scenes**. They look for things such as fingerprints and hairs.

This is called **trace evidence**.

CHAPTER 2

AT THE CRIME LAB

The crime scene investigators take the trace evidence to the **crime lab**.

Powerful microscopes help the crime lab technicians look at tiny bits of evidence.

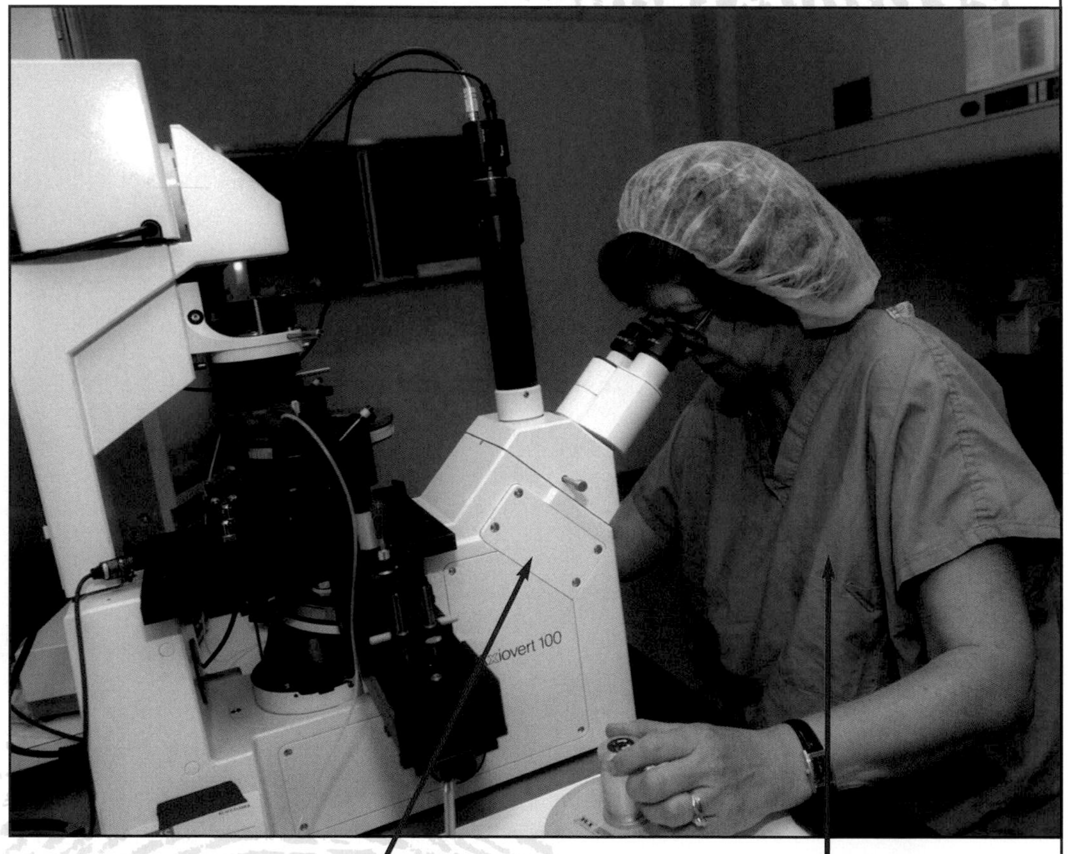

Microscope

Crime lab technician

A crime lab technician looks at dust found at the crime scene.

When two objects touch, tiny **particles** such as dust get moved from one object to another.

Dust from Suspect A

Dust on crime scene floor

Dust from Suspect B

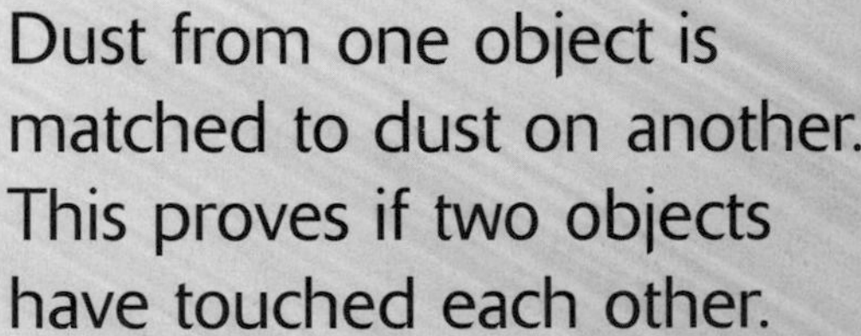

Dust from one object is matched to dust on another. This proves if two objects have touched each other.

RESULT

Dust from the crime scene is found on Suspect A and Suspect B.

CHAPTER 3

BLOOD TRACES

Clothes from both suspects are sent to the crime lab.

The lab technician tests them.
She is looking for traces of the victim's blood.

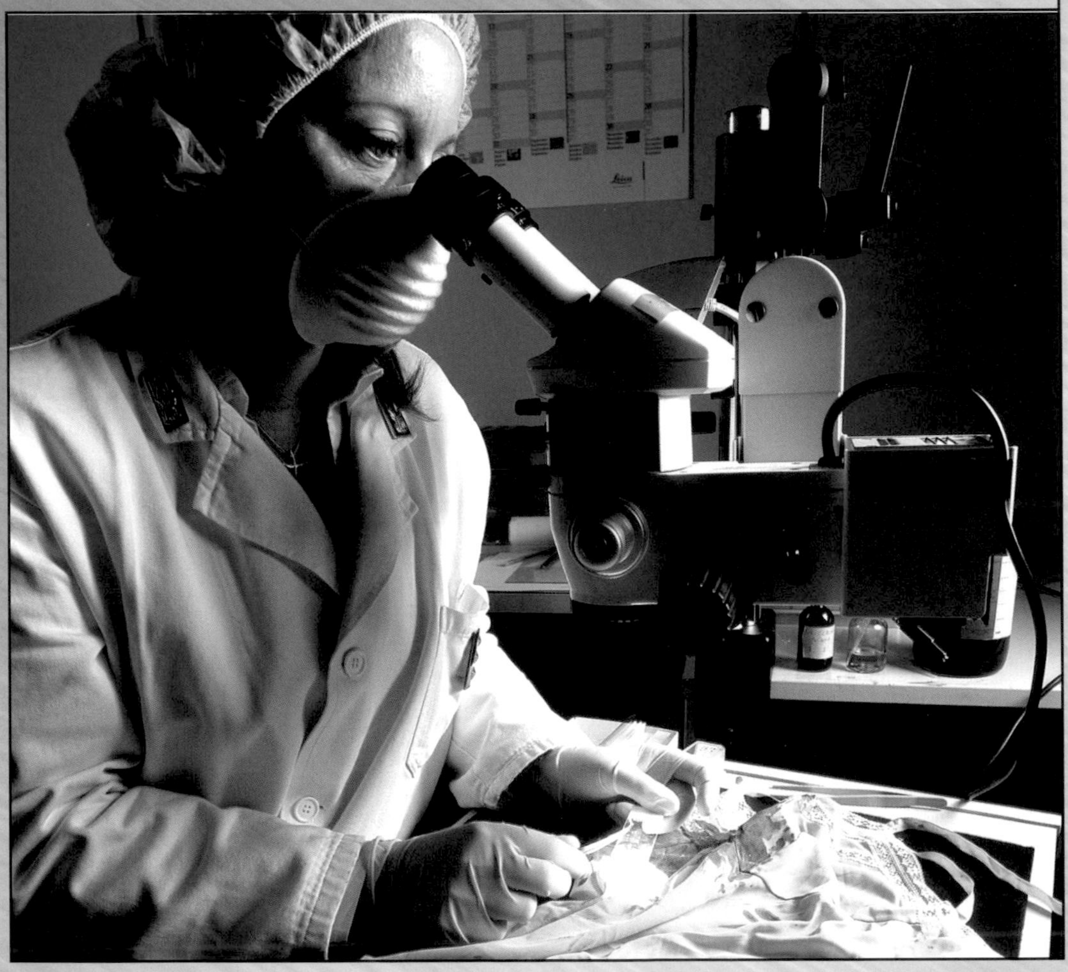

Just ONE SPOT of blood proves the suspect was at the crime scene.

Even if clothes have been washed, traces of blood can still be found.

A special chemical called Luminol is sprayed on clothes. Then the clothes are put under an **ultraviolet light**. The Luminol helps blood stains show up. The blood glows under the light.

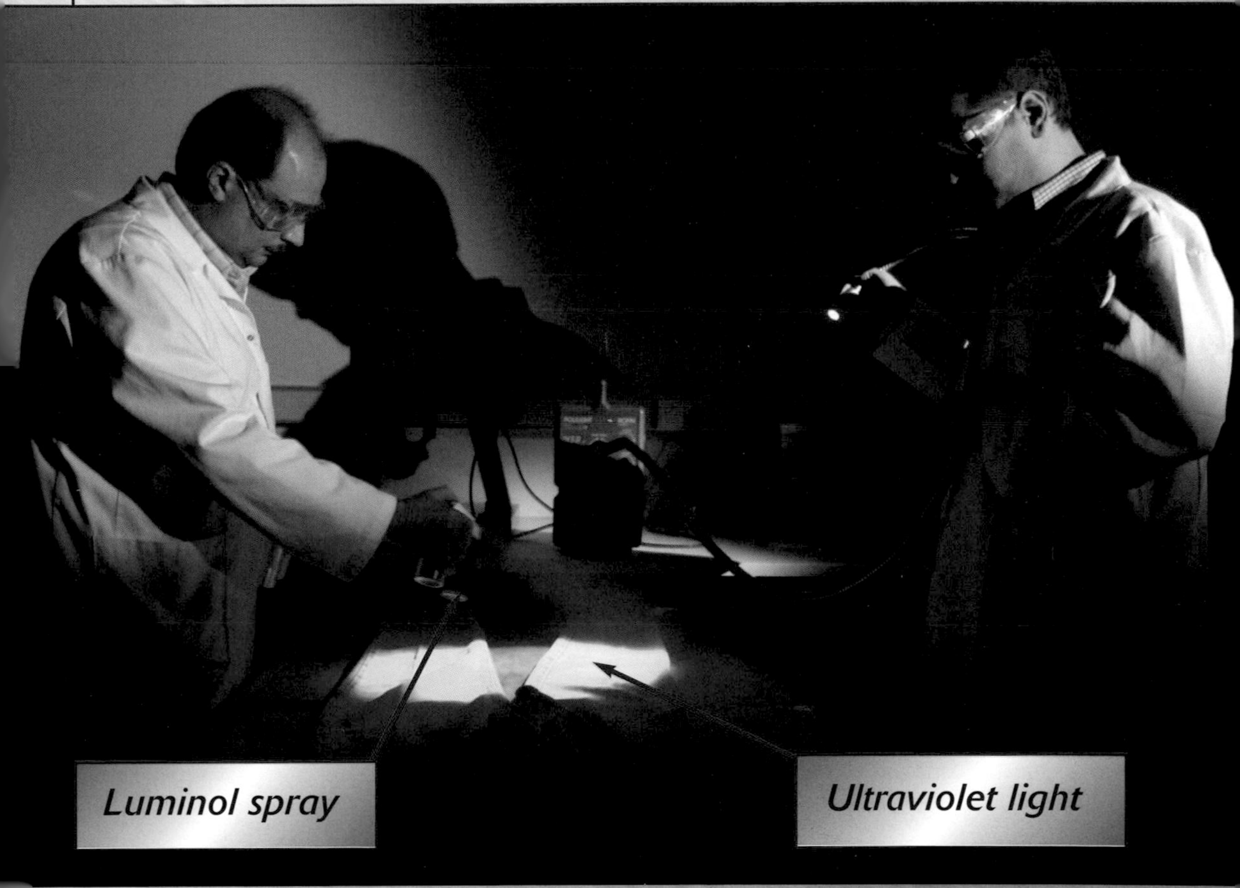

Luminol spray

Ultraviolet light

So where did the blood on the suspects come from?

DNA tests can prove if the blood came from the victim.

Cells in our blood are **unique**, just like our fingerprints! The cells contain unique information called DNA.

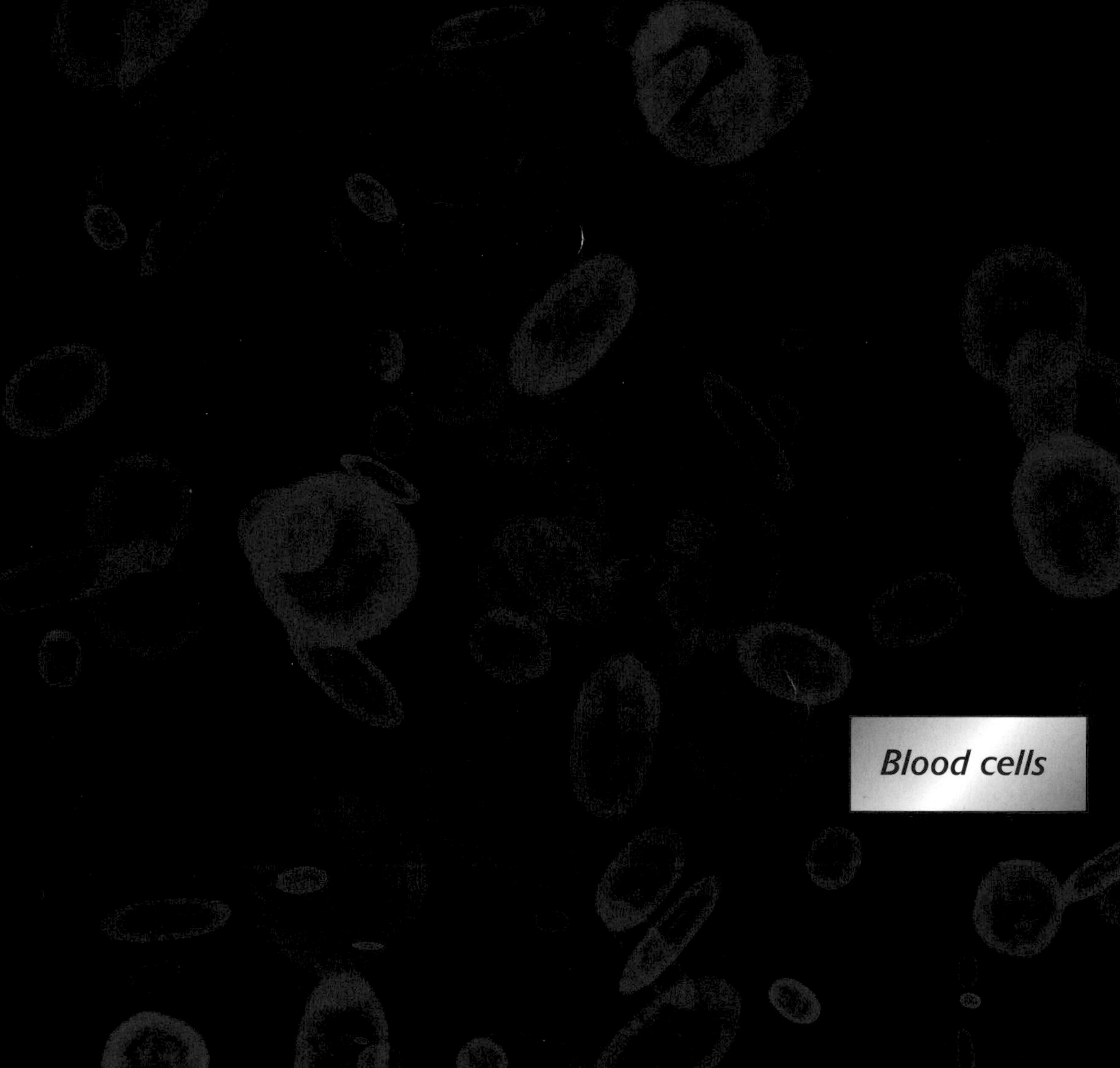

Blood cells

DNA tests are done on blood samples. Special machines "read" the DNA.

They display the information in a pattern called a **profile**.

A profile is made of the blood on the suspects' clothes. Then a profile is made of the victim's blood.

If the profiles match, it means both blood samples are from the same person.

RESULT

The blood on both suspects' clothes is from the victim.

CHAPTER 4

THE MURDER WEAPON

The police find a gun near the crime scene.

There are deposits of gunshot discharge residue (GSR) on the gun. There is the smell of gunpowder, too.

This means the gun has been fired recently.

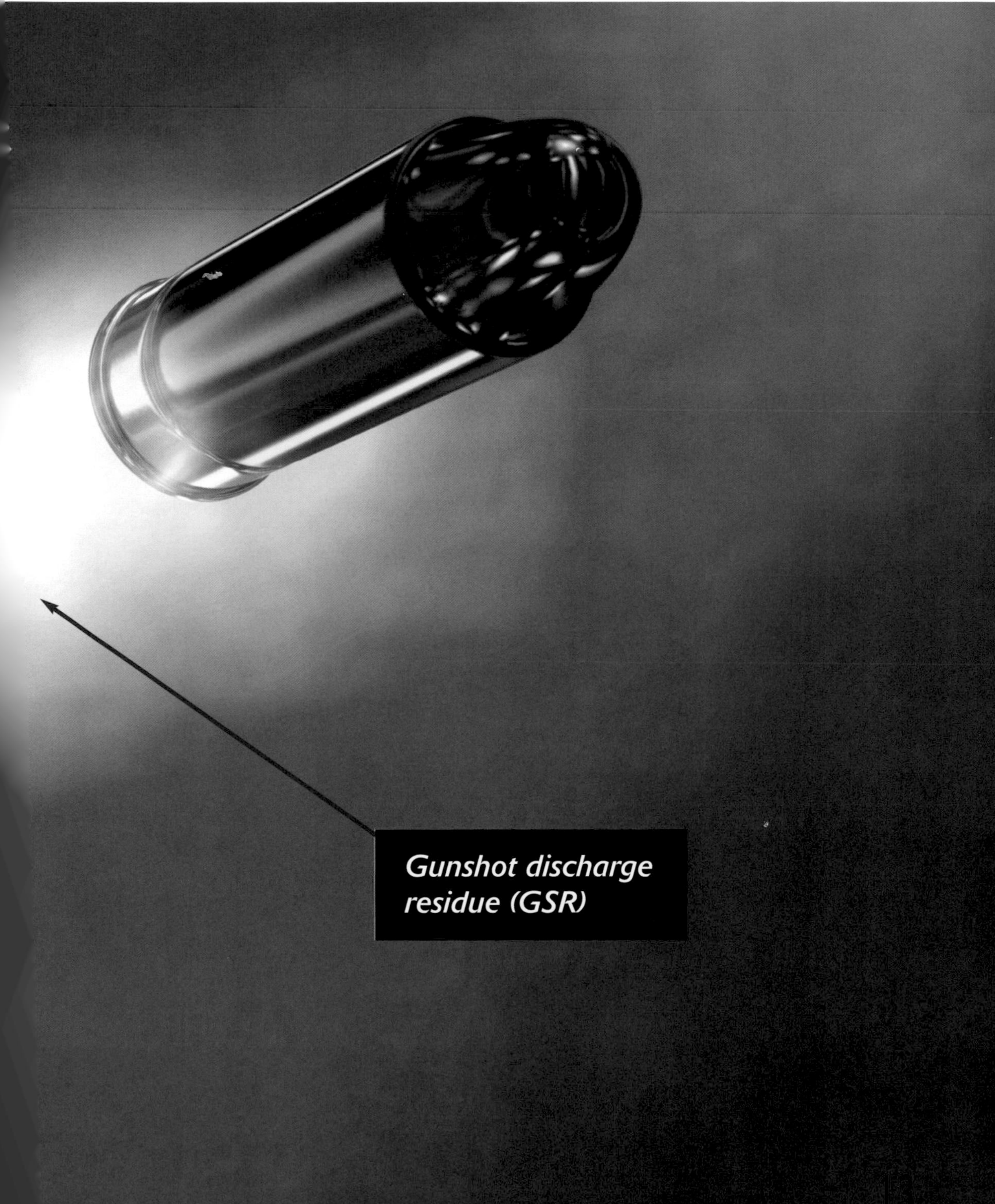

There are bullets in the victim's body.

Tiny scratches on a bullet match marks inside a gun.

The gun from the crime scene is fired by a **firearms expert**. The bullets from the gun are compared to the bullets in the dead body.

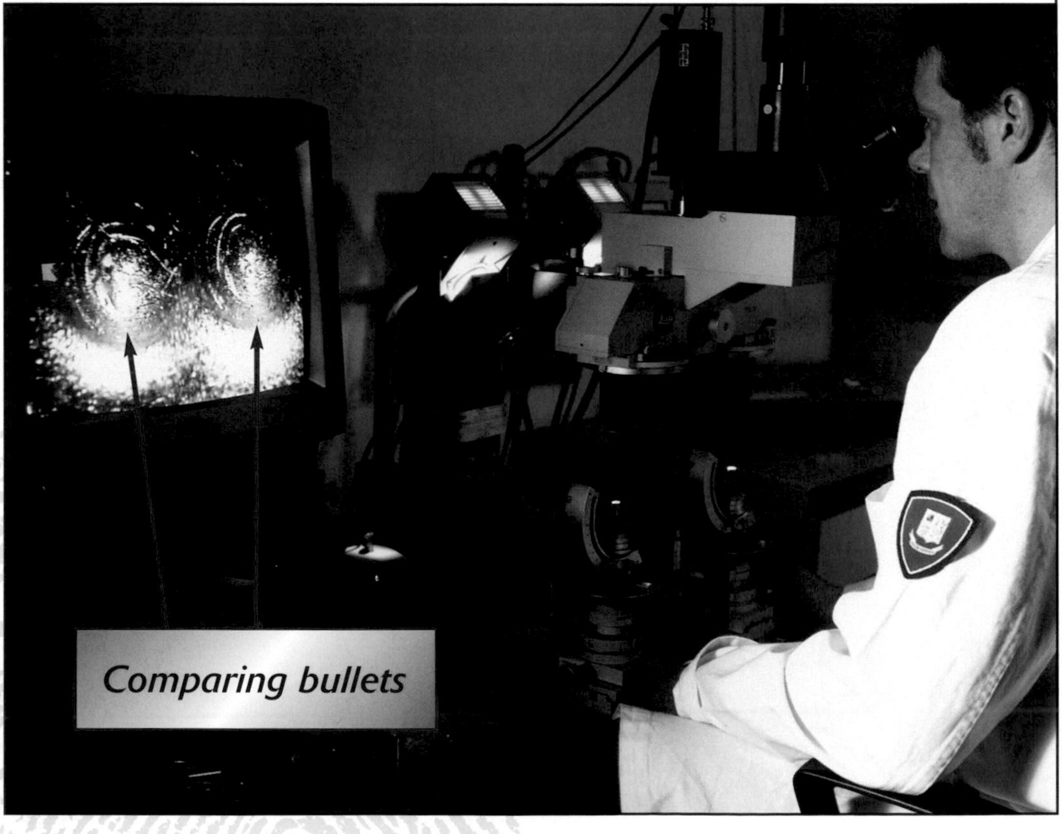

Comparing bullets

A lab technician uses a powerful microscope to compare the bullets.

The lab technician can prove if the gun fired the bullets found in the victim. But the technician cannot prove who pulled the trigger.

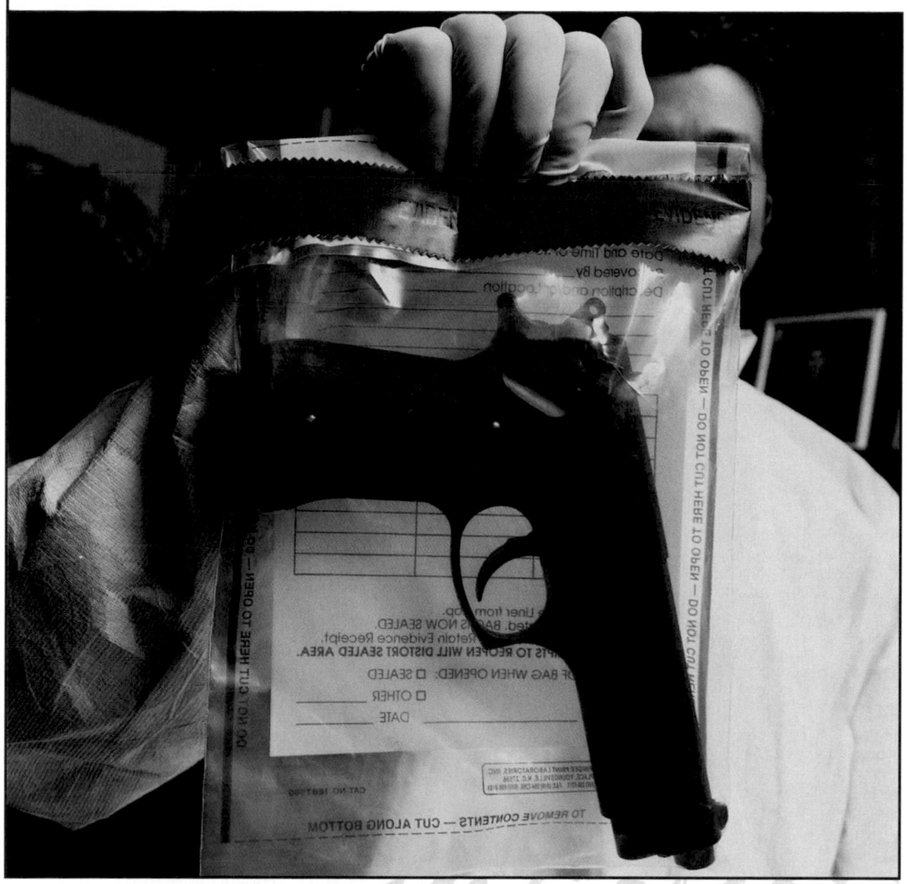

The lab technician might find gunpowder from the gun on a suspect's clothes. But it doesn't mean the suspect fired the gun. Anyone standing close to a gun when it is fired can get traces on them.

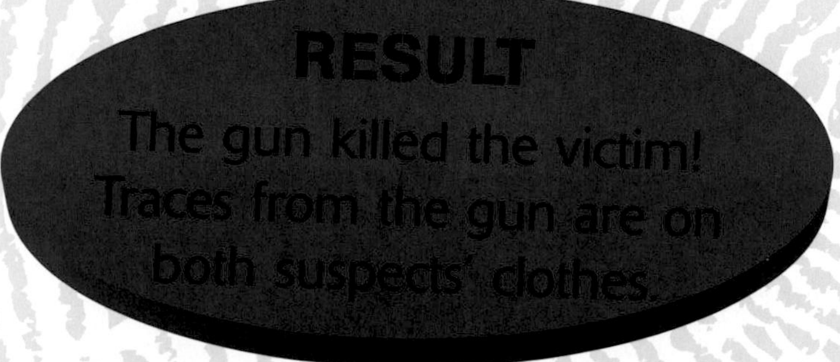

CHAPTER 5

TRACE EVIDENCE

A crime lab technician finds a fingerprint on the gun.

No two people have the same fingerprints.

Whenever you touch something, you leave a smear of grease, dust, or sweat behind.

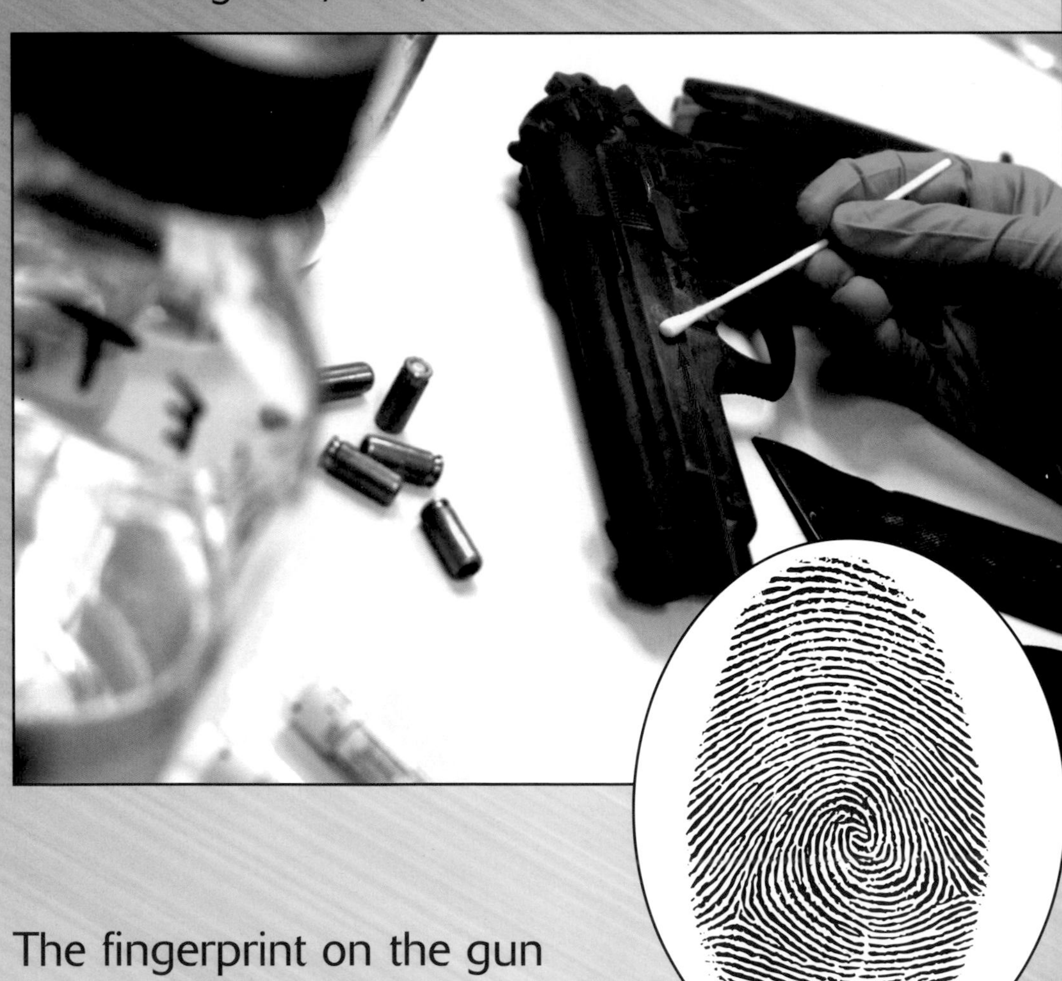

The fingerprint on the gun is matched to prints found at the crime scene.

Fingerprint on gun

These fingerprints were found at the crime scene. Can you find a match to the print on the gun?

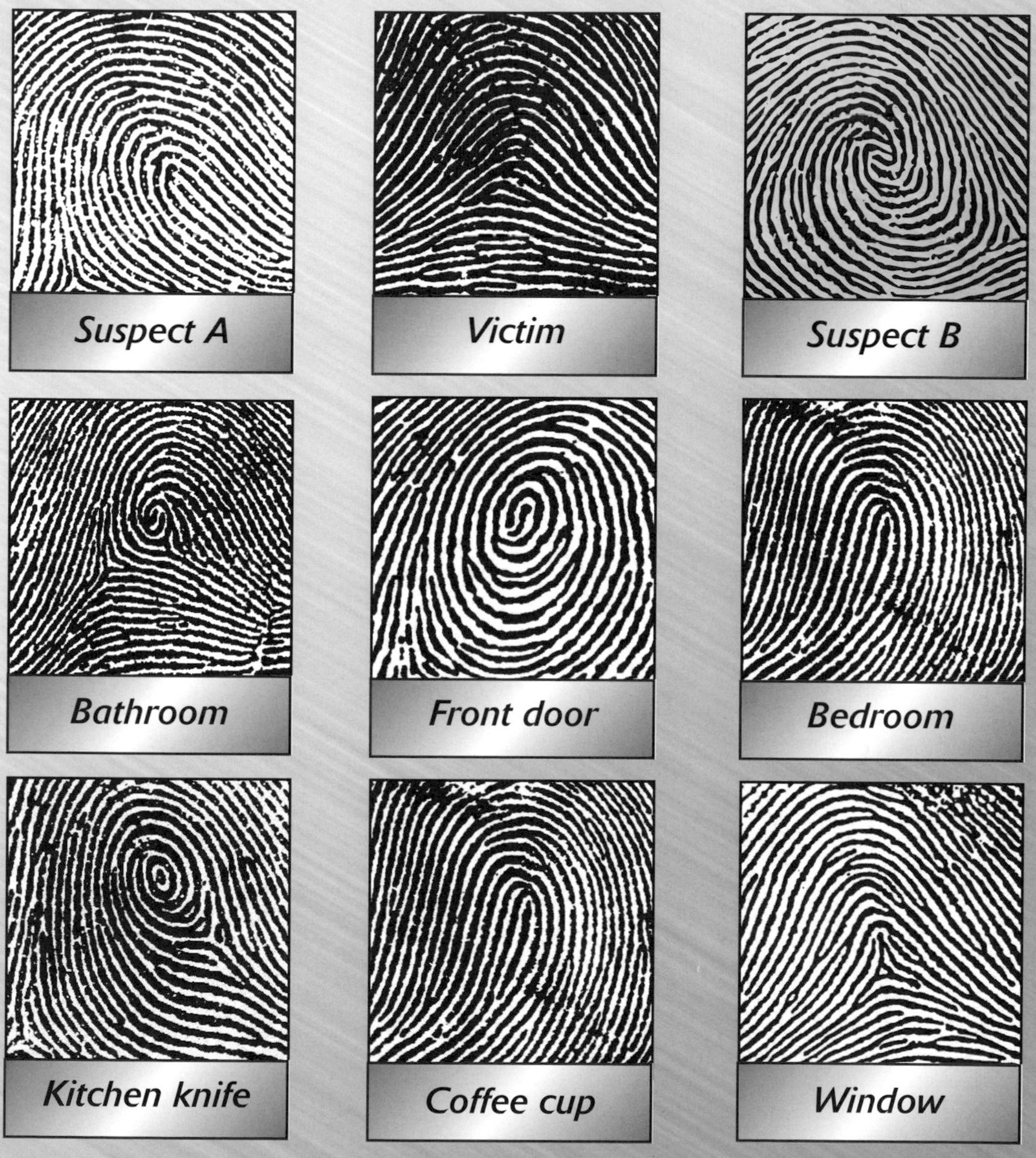

RESULT

Suspect B's fingerprint is on the gun.

Next, a lab technician examines hairs on the suspects' clothes.

Hairs are examined under a microscope.
The first job is to make sure it's human hair.
Then the lab technician finds out who the hairs belong to.

This is a close-up of dog hairs. Each hair has an outer layer of overlapping scales.

The technician examines the hair root and measures its **diameter** and length. The technician also looks at the pattern of the scales and the color of the hair.

DNA tests are also done on the hairs.

RESULT

Hairs on Suspect B's clothes came from the victim.

This is a close-up of human hairs. The human hairs look very different from dog hairs.

The killer got into the victim's house by breaking a window.

A lab technician finds glass on Suspect A's jeans.

No glass is exactly the same. A chemical test will show if the glass on the jeans is made exactly like the window glass.

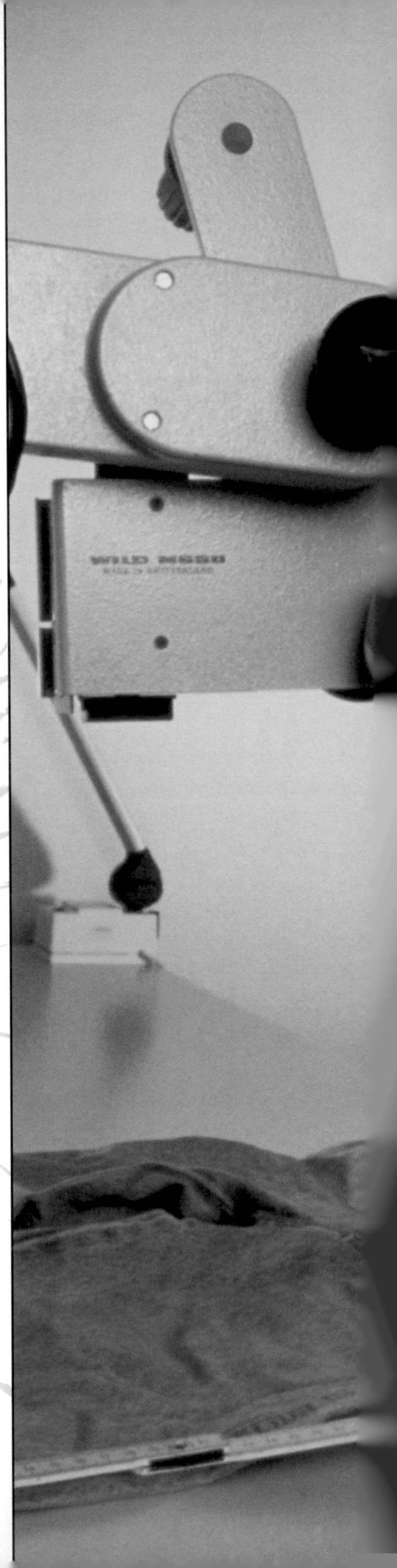

RESULT
The glass from Suspect A came from the window at the crime scene.

CHAPTER 6

A PUZZLE

A lab technician looks at the victim's socks under a microscope.

The socks are full of tiny specks. They are grains of **pollen**.

Tests show the pollen may have come from an ash tree.

But there are NO ash trees near the crime scene.

The police visit the homes of the two suspects. There is an ash tree in Suspect B's garden.

The police search around the tree and find a piece of chewing gum under the tree.

The crime lab technicians test the chewing gum for **saliva**.

The saliva contains the victim's DNA!

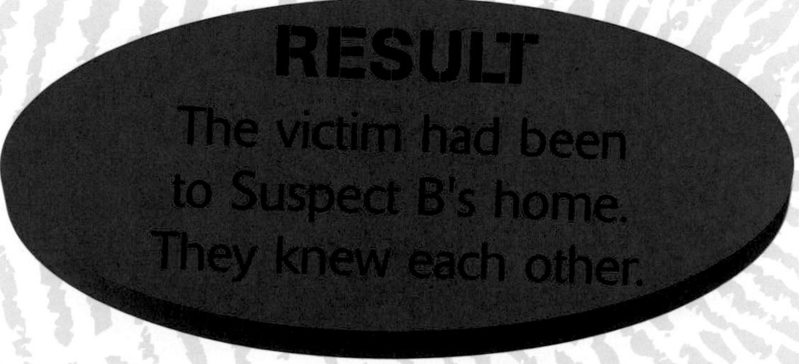

Both suspects swear they have never been near the victim's house.

But then the CSIs find a shoeprint in the mud by the broken window.

They make a mold of the shoeprint and take it to the lab.

mold of shoeprint

A lab technician matches the mold to the suspect's shoe.

Suspect's shoe

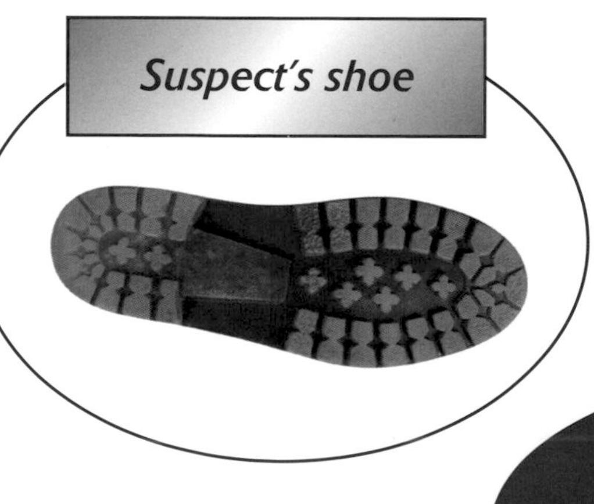

RESULT

Suspect B's left shoe made the shoeprint.

Suspect B must be guilty!

But then the lab technician finds more trace evidence. Inside Suspect B's shoe are tiny **fibers**.

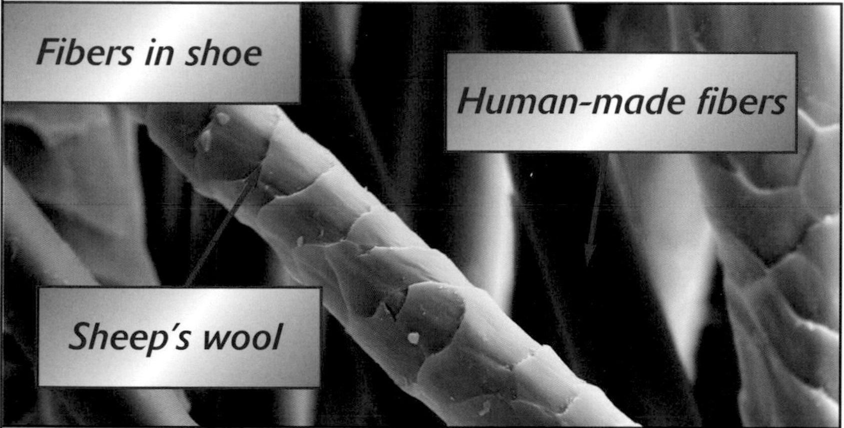

The lab technician looks at the fibers under a microscope.

Suspect A's socks

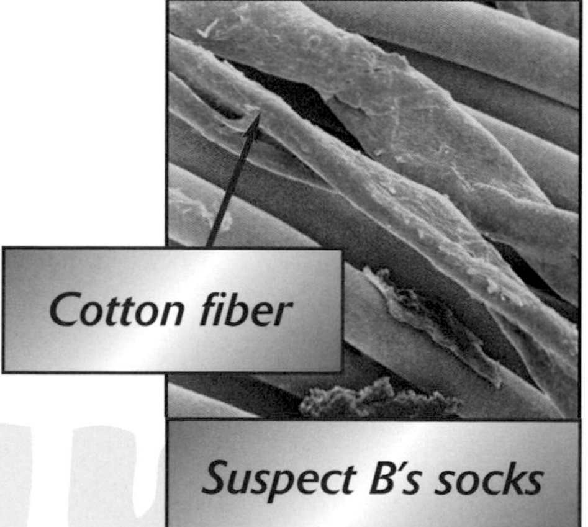

Suspect B's socks

The fibers do not match Suspect B's socks. They match the socks of Suspect A!

CHAPTER 7

FINAL PROOF

Suspect A says again he never met the victim. The police look at a bite on his arm. He says it's a dog bite.

They photograph the bite and send pictures to the crime lab. The lab technician has a theory.

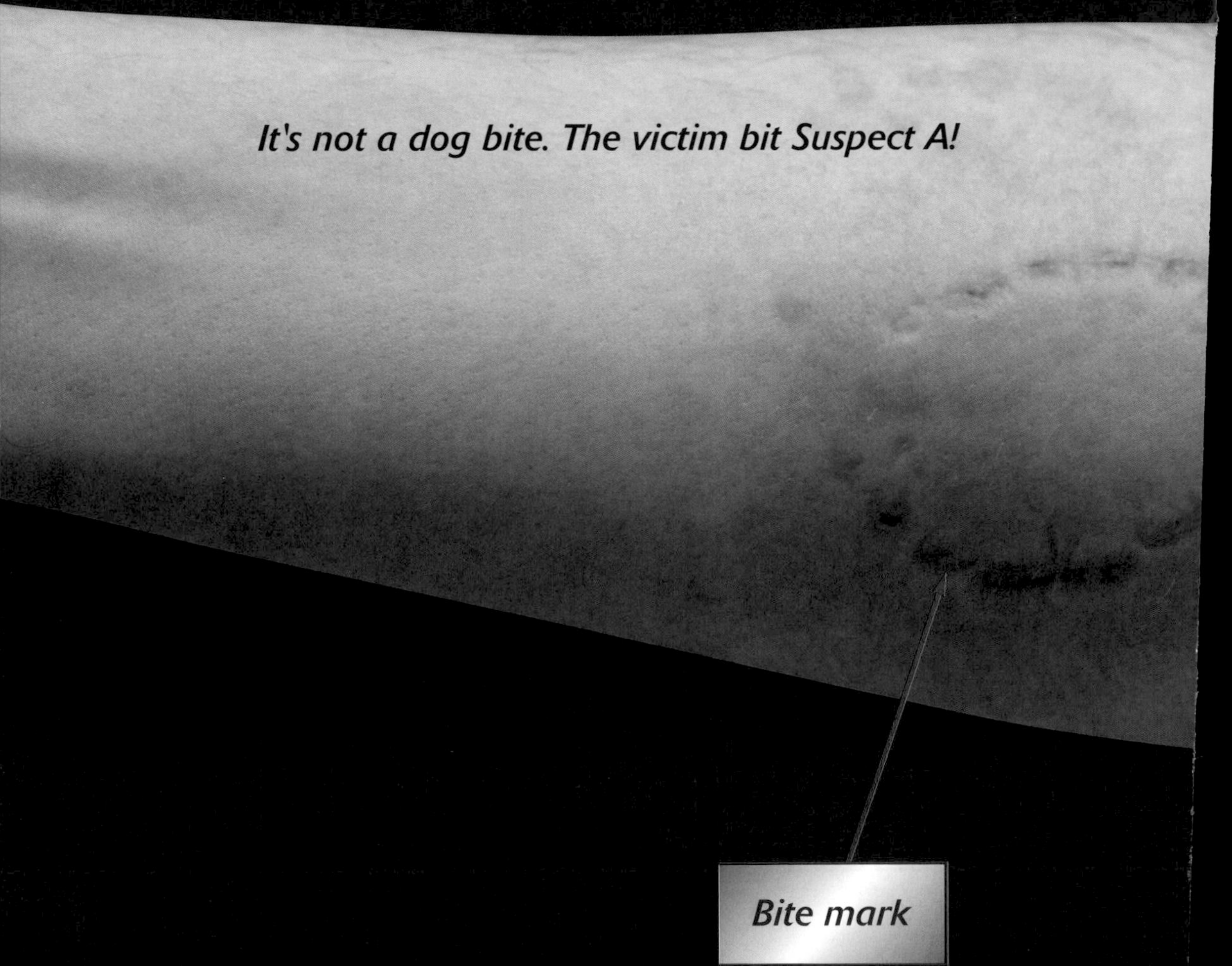

It's not a dog bite. The victim bit Suspect A!

Bite mark

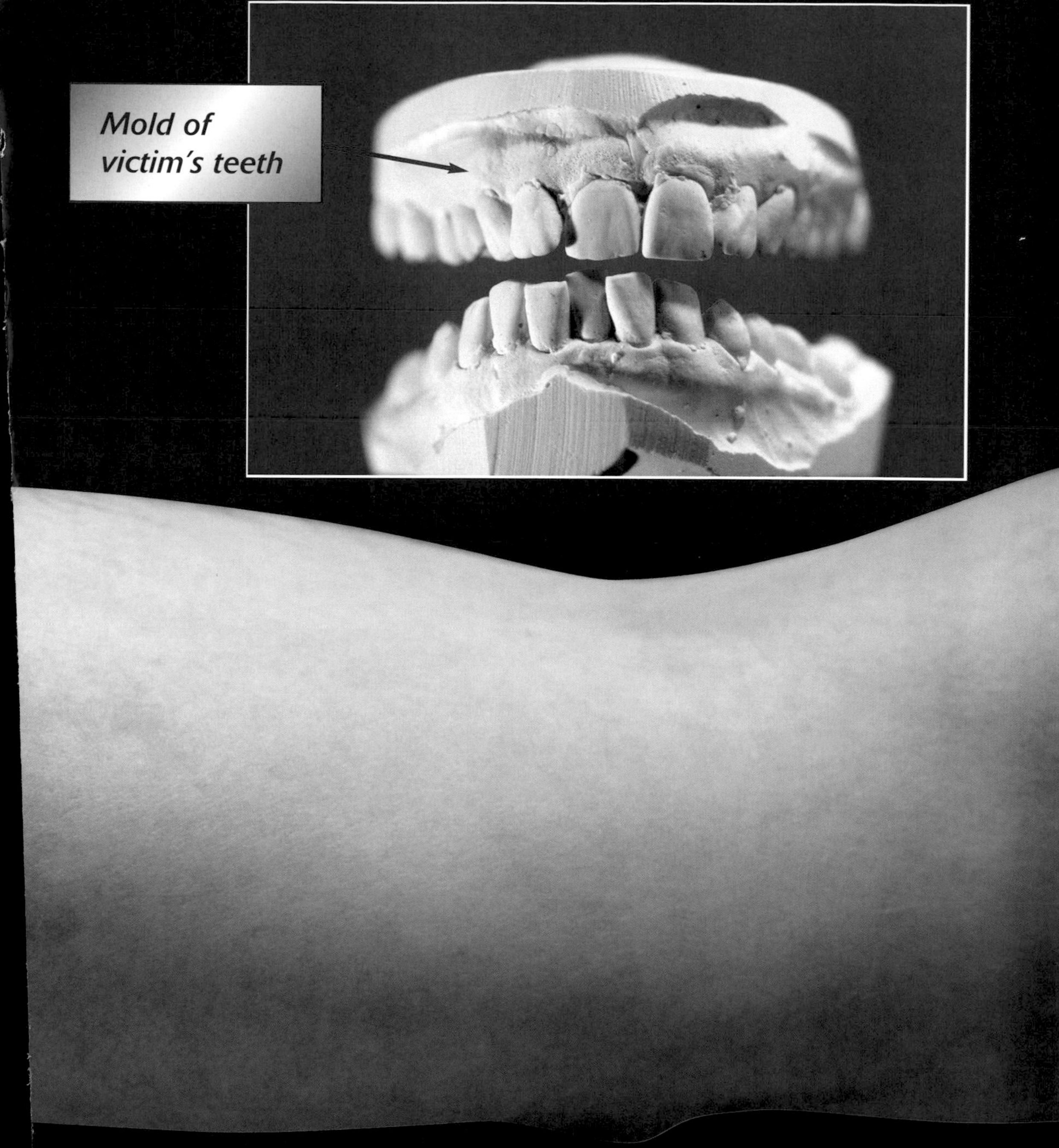

The crime lab make a mold of the victim's teeth. They scan this into a computer and make a **3-D image**. The victim's teeth match the bite on Suspect A's arm.

It's not a dog bite. The victim bit Suspect A!

THE CHARGE

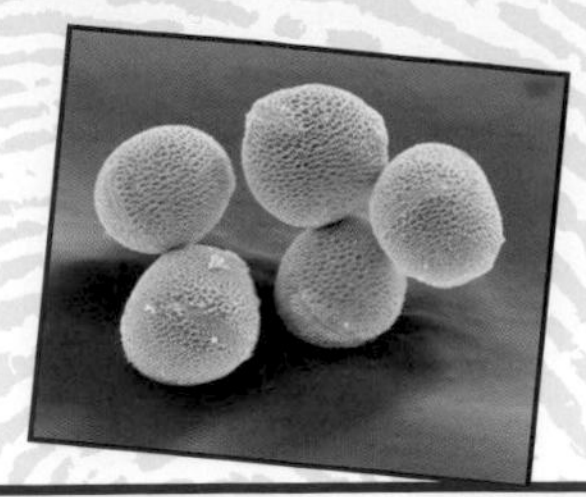

LAB REPORT: SUSPECT A

EVIDENCE	MATCH
Dust	✓
Victim's blood on clothes	✓
Gunshot discharge residue	✓
Fingerprint on gun	X
Victim's hair on clothes	X
Glass	✓
Pollen	X
Chewing gum	X
Shoeprint	X
Sock fiber	✓ in B's shoe
Bite from victim	✓

Statement:
I never knew the victim and was never at the scene. I've been **framed**!

Suspect A

Suspect A is charged with murder.

In court, Suspect A is found **guilty** of the murder.

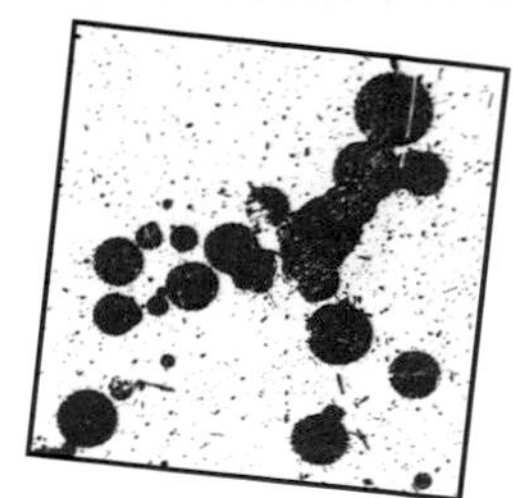

LAB REPORT: SUSPECT B

EVIDENCE	MATCH
Dust	✓
Victim's blood on clothes	✓
Gunshot discharge residue	✓
Fingerprint on gun	✓
Victim's hair on clothes	✓
Glass	X
Pollen	✓
Chewing gum	✓
Shoeprint	✓ planted
Sock fiber	X
Bite from victim	X

Statement:

I found the body and tried to help. I saw the gun and picked it up. I was scared to tell the police I knew the victim.

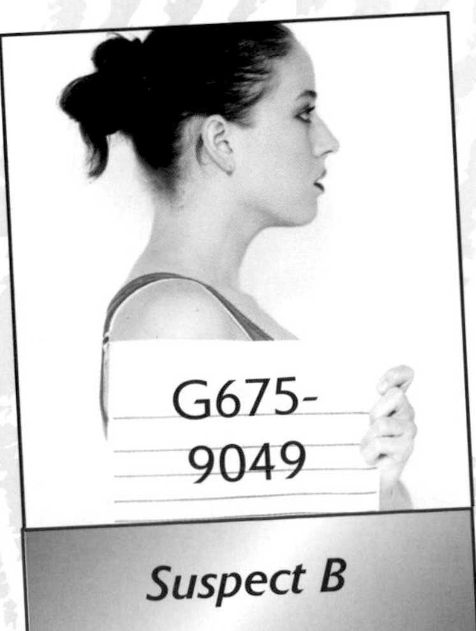

Suspect B

Suspect B was a witness to the crime.

Suspect B got evidence traces on her when she found the victim's body.

CASE SOLVED!

GLOSSARY

crime lab A laboratory with equipment that is used for scientific experiments and tests on crime-scene evidence

crime scene Any place where a crime has happened

deny To refuse to admit or accept the truth

diameter The width of a circle

DNA The special code in the center (or nucleus) of each person's cells. Our DNA makes us all unique.

evidence Facts and signs that can show what happened during a crime

fiber A tiny thread

firearms expert A scientist who tests guns and bullets

framed When a false charge is made and an innocent person is made to look as if they are guilty

guilty Having done wrong, such as committing a crime

particle A very small piece or part

pollen Fine grains like dust – made by flowers and trees

profile A visual printout of a person's DNA code

saliva A fluid made in the mouth to assist eating (spit)

suspect A person who is thought to have committed a crime

3-D image A three-dimensional computer image that gives depth and scale. 3-D images help users see a realistic object or scene from three directions.

trace A very small mark, sign, or substance that is left behind

ultraviolet light A special light that shines deep purple, making some objects glow in the dark. It is sometimes called a black light.

unique The only one of its kind

victim A person who is hurt or killed

witness Someone who saw a crime being committed or who has information about a crime

LIFE IN THE LAB

Would you like to be a crime lab technician? Here are some jobs you could do!

- **Fingerprints and impressions**
  You will analyze and compare fingerprints, footwear, and tire marks. Technicians match crime scene fingerprints with fingerprints of known criminals. They use a database that holds millions of fingerprint records.

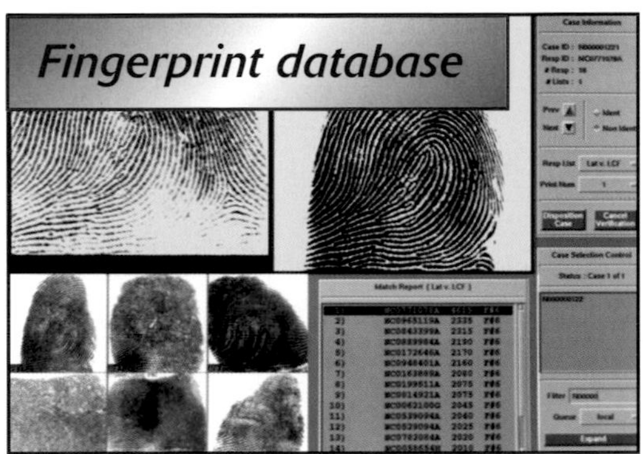

- **Toxicology**
  You will analyze poisons and substances such as drugs and alcohol. If a victim has been poisoned, you will test samples of hair, blood, and skin.
- **Firearms**
  You will identify and test guns. You will work out the distance of a gunshot from a victim's wound. You will identify and compare bullets.
- **Documents**
  You will detect forgery and changes to important papers or letters. You will compare samples of handwriting and reconstruct destroyed documents.

Is this the job for you?

CRIME ONLINE

WEBSITES about Crime Scene Investigation:

www.fbi.gov/kids/6th 12th/6th 12th.htm
How the FBI investigates crimes

www.howstuffworks.com/csi5.htm
All about the world of CSI

library.thinkquest.org/04oct/00206/tte_every_criminal_leaves_a_trace.htm
"Let evidence reveal the truth"

http://www.pbs.org/wgbh/nova/sheppard/analyze.html
Learn more about DNA and solve a crime.

Publisher's note to educators and parents:
Our editors have carefully reviewed these websites to ensure that they are suitable for children. Many websites change frequently, however, and we cannot guarantee that a site's future contents will continue to meet our high standards of quality and educational value. Be advised that children should be closely supervised whenever they access the Internet.

INDEX

Printed in the U.S.A.